THIS CANDLEWICK BOOK BELONGS TO:

_____

_____

_____

Little Pinto of
MUSTANG CANYON

For Roger & Lisa & Rowan—friends of the canyon
With thanks owed to Hope Ryden, for her work   J. L.

For all the children who are captivated by wild horses   D. S. S.

First paperback edition 2007
Originally published as *Mustang Canyon*

The Library of Congress has cataloged the hardcover edition as follows:
London, Jonathan, date.
Mustang Canyon / by Jonathan London ; illustrated by Daniel San Souci. — 1st ed.
p.   cm.
Summary: A young mustang is separated from its mother when a plane sweeps over the canyon.
ISBN 978-0-7636-1554-3 (hardcover)
1. Mustang—Juvenile fiction. [1. Mustang—Fiction. 2. Animals—Infancy—Fiction. 3. Horses—Fiction.] I. San Souci, Daniel, ill. II. Title.
PZ10.3.L8534 Mu 2002   [E]—dc21   2001025680

ISBN 978-0-7636-3513-8 (paperback)

10 9 8 7 6 5 4 3 2 1

Printed in China

This book was typeset in Quercus Hard and Block Heavy.
The paintings were done with Windsor Newton watercolors on DeArches 300 lb. hot press paper.
The artist used Prismacolor pencils to highlight the colors of the horses and the desert landscapes.

Candlewick Press
2067 Massachusetts Avenue
Cambridge, Massachusetts 02140

visit us at www.candlewick.com

Little Pinto of
MUSTANG
CANYON

JONATHAN LONDON
illustrated by DANIEL SAN SOUCI

CANDLEWICK PRESS
CAMBRIDGE, MASSACHUSETTS

Out of the blue haze of evening
comes a soft whinny as a mother mare
nuzzles her foal.

Less than a day old, the little pinto tries to stand.
Sits. Tries again, wobbling, poking his nose beneath her,
pushing for milk.

Three weeks later, Little Pinto
is ready to nibble grass.
The band of mustangs is free to travel.
The herd master, the old white-faced stallion, will lead them.

Pintos, bays, sorrels, roans—
the herd races across the high desert flats,
searching for those hard-to-find patches of green.

Near the back, Little Pinto struggles to keep up.

Summer is near and the heat bores down.
The mustangs are getting thirsty.
Old White Face leads them along the rimrock,
then down into a canyon
toward the sweet smell of water.

While the mares, colts, and fillies
drink at the river's edge,
Old White Face stands guard,
alert for any sign of danger.
Little Pinto drinks deep,
his mother by his side.

Then around a boulder come a scent
and a sound.

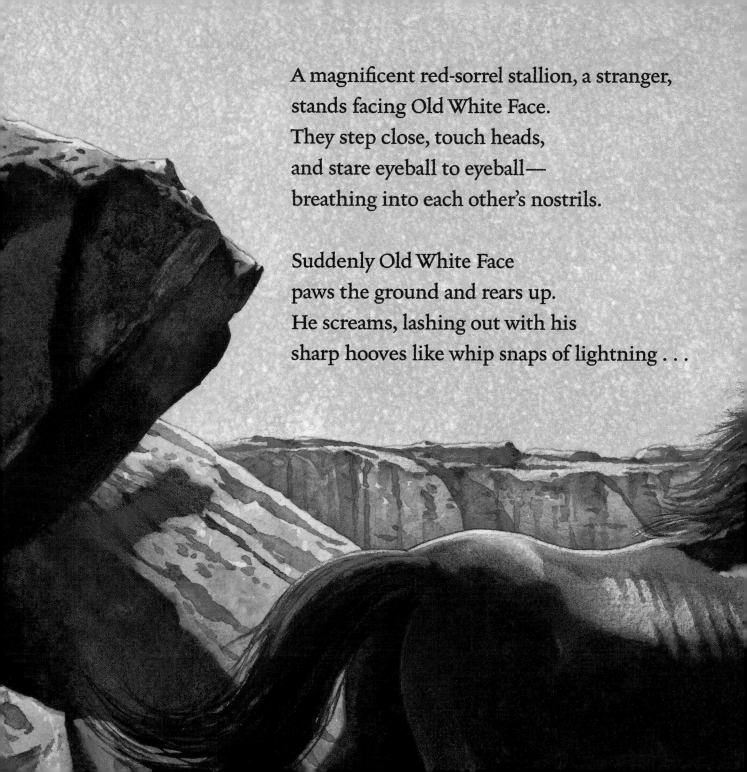

A magnificent red-sorrel stallion, a stranger,
stands facing Old White Face.
They step close, touch heads,
and stare eyeball to eyeball—
breathing into each other's nostrils.

Suddenly Old White Face
paws the ground and rears up.
He screams, lashing out with his
sharp hooves like whip snaps of lightning . . .

and the rogue stallion whirls and flees.
Old White Face chases him briefly,
then swerves back, sweating and blowing,
prancing before his band.

But something else is coming.
A low drone sounds in the distance,
and the canyon walls vibrate.
The sound grows louder. It's getting closer.

A plane! Flying low. Wings tilted,
sun bursting off its sides.
Old White Face's mane bristles
as memories stir.
Planes have come before—
to round up mustangs.

Ears back, neck arched, he snorts a warning
and the harem scatters behind him,
bolting back down the canyon
toward the river.

Far behind the others, Little Pinto scrambles
on bony legs, his mane flying
and his tail flat out behind him.

The herd is a cloud of dust,
pounding through the canyon, and the roar
of the engine fills his bones
with dread.

Little Pinto slips on loose rock.

He stumbles—the wind tearing out of him—
and the next moment,
he's in the air . . .

falling, falling, crashing
into the white terror of the river.

Little Pinto kicks bottom.
His teeth chomp for air,
but icy water gags him.
He skims off boulders
and is swept thrashing
around holes in the rapids,
haystacks of white power . . .

all the way
to the far side.

He staggers out
and stands shivering and ragged,
dripping and all alone
on a rock shelf.

The roar of the plane has vanished.
All he hears now
is the softer roar of the river.

Then, on the opposite bank,
a whinny . . . a white face appears
between boulders.
His father!
And beside Old White Face, his mother!
Mama Pinto shakes her mane . . .

and plunges in.
She is coming. She is coming.

Soon Mama Pinto is beside her colt, nuzzling him, nickering, and Little Pinto dances, then nudges for milk. The whole band is waiting.

When Little Pinto is finished drinking, he and his mother
plunge back into the river and thrash across to safety.

That evening, the mustangs—
the wind-racers, the wind-drinkers—
gallop along the rimrock and the desert flats,
toward the blue haze of the mountains,
wild with life.

And Little Pinto is right with them.
Someday he will lead
a band of his own.

AFTERWORD

Sky Dogs, Spirit Dogs, Elk Dogs. The Plains Indians used these names to describe the mustangs, or wild horses, that have lived in North America for five hundred years. Our term, mustang, may have come from *mesteño,* the Spanish word for "a stray."

Paleontologists believe that horses originated in North America about three million years ago and spread into Asia over the Bering Straits, a land bridge that connected the two continents at that time. Slowly, horses traveled to every other continent except Australia. But for some unknown reason, horses disappeared from North America about ten thousand years ago. It was not until the 1500s that the Spanish conquistadors brought their breed of Arabian horses, the Spanish Barbs, back to America. These hearty horses were hoisted into slings and crossed the ocean by boat.

Soon wild horses—descendants of the Spanish Barb—again roamed the West. By the early 1700s, their population had grown to two million. Mustangs revolutionized the lives of the Plains Indians, who, until then, had hunted for buffalo on foot.

Like most wild creatures, wild horses fear man above all other enemies. After the coming of more European settlers to the West in the nineteenth century, hundreds of thousands of wild horses were rounded up to be used as cow ponies, or were shot by cattlemen who wanted grazing land cleared for their stock. In the twentieth century, mustangs were rounded up—sometimes by plane—to be slaughtered for chicken feed and hides. Out of two million, only seventeen thousand were left by 1971, when Congress finally made it a federal crime to kill or remove a wild horse living on public range lands. The law now recognizes that "wild free-roaming horses and burros are living symbols of the historic and pioneer spirit of the West."

To see them in the wild is to experience the spirit of freedom.

GLOSSARY

The numbers in parentheses refer to the numbered horses in the illustration above.

BAND: A group of animals

BAY: A reddish brown horse with dark mane and tail (10)

COLT: A young male horse

FILLY: A young female horse

FOAL: A young horse, especially under one year

HAREM: A group of female animals following one dominant male

MARE: A female horse

PALOMINO: A gold-colored horse with white mane and tail (11)

PINTO: A horse marked with patches of white and another color (1, 3, 6, 8, 9, 13)

ROAN: A reddish brown horse whose coat is mixed with gray or white; may also be a gray-colored horse whose black coat is mixed with white (5)

SORREL: An orange- or chestnut-colored horse, often with a light-colored mane and tail (7, 12)

STALLION: A male horse

STANDARD BROWN: A horse whose brown mane and tail match its body (2, 4)